AN ANATOMY
OF THE NIGHT

AN ANATOMY
OF THE NIGHT

Clayton Eshleman

BlazeVOX [books]
Buffalo, NY

An Anatomy Of The Night by Clayton Eshleman
Copyright © 2011

Published by BlazeVOX [books]

Printed in the United States of America
Cover art by
Book design by Geoffrey Gatza

First Edition
ISBN: 978-1-60964-095-8
Library of Congress Control Number: 2011942493

BlazeVOX [books]
76 Inwood Place
Buffalo, NY 14209

Editor@blazevox.org

publisher of weird little books

BlazeVOX [books]

blazevox.org

2   4   6   8   0   9   7   5   3   1

BlazeVOX

Acknowledgments

My gratitude to Ron Padgett who read the first and penultimate drafts of this summational work, and made very useful editorial suggestions, nearly all of which I accepted and incorporated. Padgett's participation in my working through the multiple strategies involved in realizing this poem was a true gesture of comradely display.

AN ANATOMY
OF THE NIGHT

[1]

The sky a bath   incestuous
                    dissolving urn and tower
         strewn petals gust and blend   Whitman arched by
                              his menstrual harp,
         vermilion moon scarves,   surf resounding,
swim through our serpent-paneled spines,
stages interlocked and released by fountains rising from
         when we were masts

                         Earth
         pink and quilted with tufts of violet grass,
      miniver and rose
                         I glimpse Wilhelm Reich
                the last night of his life,   November 3, 1957
                    recumbent on a prison cot

All is alive including the death carousel I load into the projector
of my awareness

Bashō's compote of cicada-absorbed rock
Aphrodite's pudenda served on an orchid of clouds

         Graze of the night's hydra-mollusked tongue

[2]

spider

All night long I was Argiope
    laying out draglines,   sifting
visual seam for word spore,   dragonizing
      my agon,   working
   star wreathes into phrase fairs,   excreting
    sermon fuel, thread coals,
      a shadow self in shaman sores…

    The queen's pedipalp tapped my shoulder,
     plumbed my marrow flora
                "Come,
   let us irritate the vessels of the earth—
    they shall distill strange wine"

[3]

What is the nature of the night?

Might it be the boundless destruction of existence in the origin of
the universe?

Is it an infusion brewed of cosmic darkness, initially articulated
by those shamans who, spanning the abyss of the Fall,
reconnected, if only in vision, humankind with its animal matrix?

Is earth but a tear in mad Ophelia's mangled target eye as she
crawls the Milky Way searching eternally for the right black hole
in which to deposit the God-crisis in her being?

O light, you are oasis!

Descending / ascending, a plumb line through our minds, the _axis_
mundi longings to connect that antlered shaman buried in ice
with the morning stars all singing hosanna together.

[handwritten margin note: center of the earth that connect earth & heaven]

Is there a basic dream?

An animal dives deep into primal waters, brings up earth...
I tumble into a hole, turn my body into a womb; while in this
cave I begin to daub its walls,   out of my body
                    I begin to make a world...

[4]

Géza Róheim:

"The ancestor of the [Siberian] Yakuts is called 'The Lonely Man.'
He lives in the center of a plain in a palace with four silver-
gleaming corners, forty windows, seven stories. When he comes
out of his house he sees the tree of life. Its roots reach down to
Hades, its crown pierces the seven heavens. From under its roots
foams 'eternal water.' Cattle and game drink or lick the sap which
drips from the trees' branches and their youth and strength are
restored. The spirit of the tree is a white-haired goddess with
breasts as large as leather bags. When she leaves the tree it grows
smaller, when she re-enters it it regains its former size. This milk-
breasted goddess of the tree is actually the mother of the First
Man."

[5]

Le Combel section of the Pech Merle cave contains a Black
Goddess stone tree only partially emerged from stalactites,
fissures and folds. Possibly as early as 25,000 B.P., Cro-Magnon
people identified and marked this proto-World Tree.

Her broad, short trunk has a vertical cleft, widening near the
base into a triangular hole. At the top of the trunk, out of the
chamber ceiling, pod-shaped stalactites proliferate. Under two of
these pods, along the cleft, the stalactitic mass seems to liquefy
and descends, icicling across the triangular hole, fusing with the
molten stone which appears to be emerging from the hole.

Cro-Magnons daubed manganese on a dozen or so of the pods,
turning them into blackened breasts, the trunk into a torso, the
fissured torso into monstrous trunk-legs and the triangular hole
into a seeping vulva.

These people envisioned all of this and more, for they marked
both upper sides of her trunk torso and the top of her stalactitic
clitoris with large, red-ochre disks: rotating anointments,
menstrual suns.

The stone river flowing out of her vulva conjures wise blood, a
proto-Styx, life-giving *aurr,* nectar of blood and honey—her
trunk: Yggdrasil, the Qabalistic Tree of Life.

Tracers 1

Midnight: out our bedroom window across the neighbors'
driveway through black walnut tree branches into two yellow
windows. Nothing moves, moves me deeply. Nothing, dwelling
in its still birth. I want a shadow play to silhouette Lilith *adams first wife*
mounting Adam, a Beanstalk to sprout from Jack-Adam's groin…
Two yellow windows thirty yards away… They hang there, ghost
garb on an invisible line…

    *

extermination camp

I stare into a ceiling where Savior is manacled to Sobibor

    *

Haunted by the last line of a poem by the Armenian poet
Nigoghos Sarafian: "To die without death, oh Lord, to be taken
from it alive, whole."

    *

Night as the mingling of those "kissing cousins," birth and death.
As the recumbent turns on his side, drawing up his knees, a cradle

begins to tremor; as the tremor becomes a rocking, bits of yellowish froth appear, isles of conception in the endlessness of non-existence. Before we were / After we are: reciprocal postings, sped on by sleep.

*

electroshock

In a letter to Jean Paulhan from the Rodez asylum, Antonin Artaud writes: "To sleep is not to slumber, but to live on the side of the dream, and not like a sleeper giving off the compiled mucus of the dream, but like a fiend seeking itself, contrary to any consciousness of wakefulness, in that sort of terebrant immanence, in that space of unfathomable immanence where our unconscious is woven."

[7]

James Hillman:

"Each dream is a child of Night, affiliated closely with Sleep and Death, and with Forgetting (Lethe) all that the daily world remembers. Dreams have no father, no call upwards. They come only from Night, and they have no home other than in that dark realm.

"From the psychic perspective of the underworld, only shadow has substance, only what is in the shadow matters truly, eternally. Shadow, then, in psychology is not only that which the ego casts behind, made by the ego out of its light, a moral or repressed or evil reflection to be integrated. Shadow is the very stuff of the soul, the interior darkness that pulls downward out of life and keeps one in relentless connection with the underworld.

"What is most dead and buried in each of us is the culture's neglect of Death. Hades only now begins to reappear in ominous new concerns with the limits to growth, the energy crisis, ecological pollution, ageing and dying.

"Jung's attempt to darken the Christ figure must be understood in terms of soul-making, in terms of a recognition that only through reestablishing the underworld, which it was Christ's mission to void, could the soul-making of descent and deepening toward death, so basic to the work of psychotherapy, happen at all. I understand Jung's struggle as one between two archetypal obligations: Christianism that denies the underworld, and soul-making that inevitably goes there.

"We must know the archetypal substructures which govern our reactions; we must recognize the Gods and the myths in which we are embroiled. Without this awareness, our behavior becomes wholly mythic and consciousness a delusion. When Christ was the operative myth, it was enough to know his modes and those of the Devil. We had the Christian structure for our reflection. But now that this single model of consciousness has dissociated into the root multiples which lay dormant below it and which are presented by mythology, we cannot get by without mythological reflection upon our patterns of reaction, our attitudes, our fantasies."

[8]

In a North American's thermal, carnivorous dream ground
there are cells in which jaguars are prancing. The jaws of the
    oldest gods,
bearded dragons, arch open. Out of these cuspidors, *-spittoon*
skeletal geezers are ceaselessly squirming. They carry long knives,
they're on the lookout for baby jaguar gods. These shades
still roam the Popol Vuh regions of the mind
where the Daughters of Xibalbá are ceaselessly
impregnated by spitting, decapitated heads. Ceaselessly
bearing jaguar sons. Ceaselessly avenging, ceaselessly bearing,
coming into being while losing being…
    Look:
a monkey-headed human skeleton is dancing in procession with
Gladys Eshleman, a
    dead baby Clayton on her right arm.

interacts with himself

[9]

My first "visionary" dream took place in Kyoto, 1963, when my first wife Barbara and I were living and sleeping on tatami in two rooms of a nineteenth-century Japanese house. I was daily trying to imagine what I could make of myself. Since I did not know how to generate imagination, what took place in those long mornings was often the typing out of a line or two on my typewriter, before which, cross-legged, I sat staring at the page. Grinding against latent self in the hope that an expressive self could be sparked or coaxed forth. I often had nauseating headaches and was so tense that one afternoon I passed out while reading William Blake's *Book of Urizen.*

In April of that year, I became aware of the following pattern when I stretched out on the futon to sleep: as I was about to doze off, I would hear a sharp PING that rang in or seemed struck off my forehead between my eyes (was my pineal-eye calling?). At first this "bell" was more frightening than I can describe. In an effort to escape it, I would concentrate on falling asleep. In doing so, a second thing would happen: from about fifty feet away, there was the sound of a window being slammed shut, as if someone with both hands had slammed a window as hard as possible (in our neighborhood there were no houses with Western windows). I curled tighter into myself and awaited the third phase which was a rerun of this "visionary" dream: I was in a twisting tunnel moving at high speed, head first, with a sense of impending collision, as if the only culmination could be a shattering. The tunnel was smoking, and in attempting to see through the fumes, and to get to the tunnel's end before it got to me, I would conjure my father's face. The dream would always end before I reached the tunnel's outlet. I seemed to be in the tunnel a little less time each rerun. It was as if I was on some sort of psychic hamster-belt being run through my paces night after night until a certain charge exhausted itself.

[10]

[handwritten annotations: "hour of time of birth", "benevolent nature spirits"]

My natal daemon is the Indianapolis shadow present at birth,
which dogged and occulted my existence for some twenty-two
years. Upon the discovery of imagination via poetry I began to
destroy this daemon. Although I cut it out of my solar plexus in
1963 in "The Book of Yorunomado," its elimination is a lifelong
task. The natal daemon in exultation is what Blake calls the
Selfhood, the hood worn by the self blinding it to pity and
forgiveness as well as to its own annihilation and cruelty.

This hood is like a caul kept on, as if paradise is only in the *[handwritten: amniotic membrane]*
womb and not a convexcavatious display of metaphoric
transformation.

The natal daemon can thus be sent packing but its ashes are
never blown off. Its ashes are our bones, our lightness, our
ephemerality. Thus the daemon must in banishment also be
honored. Without the Indianapolis mother-father conjunction I
would not have had the opportunity to engage in mental war.

21

[11]

What was my dream in my mother's womb?
To know my double Gemini, my Clayton double, Ira?
But I was unnamed then, of the non-named,
tuned into placenta static with the chaos of my pillow.
Did my coming into being dream at all?
If so, it was a fetal fantasy of ingesting mother morays, yes,
the eels of the mother right, the right to be,
a dream of eels wavering upright, in mother left,
wavering and reeling. Was I fearing to be left in mother as an eel?
Or to lose my eel while emerging, to be without eelity,
an ash lemon? No, I did not know this then,
I knew nothing but the daemon moray amassing in my umbilical
    tail,
the eel passing between my mother and the meander becoming
    me,
the whelping mortar, placental nog, rich with her tissue,
the gift I was taking in, her life, I was converting into a moray
    male.

[12]

Sylvia Likens, sixteen-year-old boarder into whose belly
Gertrude Baniszewski and her kids, with nails, wrote: "I am a
prostitute and proud of it." Chained to a cot in an Indianapolis
basement, you are turning sallow lily-white before my eyes, but
your awful spongy agony only *evokes* Persephone. You died in
an unidentified "underworld" with nameless monsters leeching
your brain. What call these spirally eyes I meet blinking awake?
Are these Sylvia's eyes, sister whirlpools of my own?

[13]

And how do you see my soul, I asked Nora Jaffe

"It looks to be from Arnhem Land,
a greasy red knot with filaments aspiral.
Now I see maggots on knuckle-bones—
you were entered by one.
It sank into you, a fiery amulet.
Your birth was blank and right-handed,
you're always drizzling or leaking secrets
and you throw out too many loops to the unregenerate.
This ancestor of yours was brought by a German circus to
    Switzerland
and exhibited. Before dying of ptomaine poisoning
he mated with a cage-slosher.
The infant was adopted by the Aeschelmann family
who raised the boy to be a veterinarian specializing in livestock.
While performing a Caesarean section,
he spotted the Virgin's face enwebbed with the fetus
and thereupon renounced earthly labor and delight.
He embalmed the calf fetus and prayed to it,
believing that he had made contact with a nexus uniting
the Virgin with the Beast—an unfortunate association,
for the church elders in Bern interpreted it as satanic,
proposing that Ira Aeschelmann had delivered
nothing less than the Apocalyptic Whore's fetus.
Ira was lucky to be merely banished

and spent the remainder of his seventy-seven years
as a kind of wild hermit, wandering the Alps.
Imprint is all. These circuits now
range in your shadow, ankle-chained but lively, constantly
skittering
    out of the light."

    *

The pepper-dotted room began to undulate.
I thought of the veils within "No one has lifted her veil,"
   revelation, to draw back the *velum,*
to hear dead Nora through a spiritual gate,
to see the Dogon earth naked and speechless,
without language, a fiber skirt the first word,
speech as plaited fiber, "speech lattice,"
or Christ nailed on the cross as the arrested word,
vulva as lower mouth issuing red fiber,
a many-colored Isis rainbow, net within which
my fate is entangled, where the Nora spirits can be heard.

Then I saw a black-capped facial netted "full body veil"
sitting, as if on the Kabul bridge, begging.
"No one has lifted her veil" became
"At no time have women not been oppressed."
My heart tore left and right, I tried to peel
the true from the truthful, the rainbow flashed

a central scarlet band—I knew it was the Wawilak Sisters'
    menstrual blood
circulating within rock python venom.
I saw ripples of albino babies, each with a red or silver balloon,
setting off across the rainbow bridge for
the argentine body of the moon—

the Kabul bridge beggar roared back,
burkha, menstrual never shed,
chrysalis of a monstrous anti-metamorphosis
"sewed up in a hammock, with a small opening so she can
    breathe"
—are all of us, enclosed in the world of five senses, mummified
    pupas?
The beggar hissed: "Your bars, spaced and wall-papered, allow
    some comfort and expanse.
Mine, wrapped around me, nearly cover my eyes..."

I turned and sought sleep's stagnation,
respite from the sear of intersecting planes.

Tracers 2

Gazing through the dark at the Eden eel, Thomas's "green fuse,"
Montale's "L'Anguilla," "the spark that says everything begins
when everything seems burnt out black." Eel as self-oiling word,
cry swiveling in its calling, aisle or ale, no, *eel,* phantom of
Monet's Giverny. And in the pond as well: trash, unwanted
caskets of desire, wrecked Hopkins' anapests, sludge in which
living fossils churn.

＊

Met a couple in my dream café who asked me what I'd like to
drink. I'll have an iced Lucifer, I said. Then they wanted to show
me some "low down" bars—oh, I replied, that reminds me of "the
house of blue lights," when I was a teenager in Indianapolis there
was a story circulating about this mysterious mansion out in the
countryside. At night it supposedly had a single blue light on by
the door. Kids would drive out to it, lured by that blue flame. I
drove out there once, and yes, there it was, the mansion inside
absolutely dark. Now what to do? Park and neck? What was
going on *inside*? In this dream I saw inside that long-ago
mansion: it was run by, ruled by, dogs, or were they wolves?
They had captured a woman whose body was now covered with
bites. Each time one of the animals mounted her they'd bite her as
well. "Our Lady of the Body Covered with Bites."

At the base of the sacred, this holy-dreadful (wholly dreadful) body, the tortured woman, mutilated Coatlicue inside the *Coatlicue* goddess urn.

Things do not add up; they subtract out. In the soul's countryside this animal-clustered "goddess," the blue flame around which, like circling satellites, male minds rotate, bowing and scraping, coming in for a nip now and then...

*

Once again wanting to join the yolotl heart-soul dance of the dead as we wind toward November 2. Down our marigold trail, the souls follow, sniffing for me, for you. I am thinking of Aztec excavation, the feeding of hearts to the sun; what does it mean to shovel life into source to maintain life? The Aztecs were still rooted, half-immersed in natural mash, stewing in a venomous instinctual fodder. All was blood and flower flow, Coatlicue, Mictlancihuatl... Día de muertos as the snake of America in 2009 winds through Afghanistan, as our baby snakes burst their eggs in a thousand bases "overseas"— So do I escape into this ancient Día de muertos with armadillo-shell mandolin strummers in a bald and splendid din.

[15]

O night, black wet-nurse of the golden stars!

That inspired by the nebulae in the endlessness surrounding us,
poetry might become prodigious, peregrine.

That imagination might engage the wonder of galactic imagery, as,
like the En Sof of hydrogen, it bubbles and wanes in me,
microscopic doodad.

The poem as test tube. To mix dark rose gas cliffs with swan-
snakes of exploding cotton light, orange bonfired skulls wrapped
in lit white wire…

And then to descend to those deepest trenches, the ones with
siphonophores, copepods, glass octopi, bloody-belly comb jelly
and armored sea robins—can we introduce them to Charon as he
circles Pluto?

The hell that is man mesmerizes as if to keep the mind mantised
on grief and torture, bent upon ourselves, panting after beauty,
when like astral sharks we should be cruising the Sombrero
Galaxy,

or the Eagle Nebula: trillion-mile-long towers of molecular
hydrogen rising, horned and nippled stalagmites trailing belts of
turquoise blood,

or the Carina Nebula: scorching ultraviolet radiation shredding pinpoint stars in an amassing flux of blue and rust giraffe necks, layered imploding simian craniums—

Is there interpenetration? Am I inspected not only by the eye of Muriel Rukeyser but by that of a Crowned jewel squid?

> "Press close barebosomed night! Press close magnetic
>   nourishing night!
> Night of south winds! Night of the large few stars!
> Still nodding night! Mad naked summer night!
>
> Smile, for your lover comes!"

Nearly one hundred years after the 1855 *Leaves of Grass,* in *Cosmic Superimposition* Wilhelm Reich, starting with the superimposition of two organisms or energy systems in the sexual embrace, moved to the superimposition of two orgone energy particles in the formation of matter, the development of galaxies, hurricanes, and the aurora borealis.

"Before there was any life, there was the streaming of cosmic orgone energy. When climatic conditions were sufficiently developed on the planet, life began to appear, most likely in the form of primitive plasmatic flakes... From these flakes, single-cell organisms developed over the aeons. Now, the cosmic orgone energy not only was flowing in the vast galactic spaces, but also in tiny bits of membranous matter, caught within membranes and therefore flowing, still in a spiraling fashion, within these membranes, following a *closed* system of flow.

"The fright which overcomes man still in our time when he thinks about himself; the general reluctance to think at all; the whole function of repression of emotional functions of the Self; the powerful force with which man resists knowledge about himself; the fact that for millennia he investigated the stars but not the inside of his own organism; the panic that grips the witness of orgonomic investigations at the core of man's existence; the fervent ardor with which every religion defends the unreachability and unknowability of God, which clearly represents nature *within* man, and many other facts speak a clear language regarding the terror which is connected with the deep experience of the Self."

[16]

Imaginal love
incorrigibly infected by violence,
           the damnation strut in the human,
fuse of extinction   formless horizon:
     now the daily telepathy

I listen to Caryl breathe.
               Why cannot her being
bless the world? Bless it to awaken from the doomcraft
               that is religion—

The dark sloughs its "d" and the ark of dawn,
first in my heart, then in the fuzzy edge of the window
   blind,
reveals Caryl's recumbent profile.

Blind edge, road of awe, world axis that allows me to
   contemplate her breathing.

[17]

A. Alvarez:

"Nobody knows for certain when man first produced fire mechanically. The archeologists believe there were fire-makers in China 350,000 years ago, in Europe by 250,000 BC, in Africa and West Asia 50,000-100,000 years ago. According to William T. O'Dea, who wrote the most authoritative book on the subject, fire-making by using sparks from flint and pyrites on tinder probably came before the other ancient method of rubbing hardwood against softwood (the hardwood powders the softwood to make tinder and the friction between the two creates heat), because the latter 'implies a rather more advanced stage of tool manipulation.' What is not in doubt is that, until about one hundred years ago, the only source of artificial light was fire: millennia of fire, scraps of flame in the darkness of prehistory, fragile, easily extinguished, infinitely comforting. For ancient man, whose night was full of terrors, God's first triumph was always a triumph over darkness:

"And God said, Let there be light.

"And God saw the light, that it was good: and God divided the light from the darkness.

"What you see is what you know, and what can be heard of felt or smelled but not seen is terrifying because it is formless. There are

only two ways to make night tolerable: by lighting it artificially
and by sleep which shuts down the senses."

> The first words were mixed with animal fat,
> wounded men tried to say who did it.
> The group was the rim of a to-be-invented wheel,
> their speech was spokes, looping over
> around, the hub of the fire, its silk of *us,*
> its burn of *them,* bop we dip, you dip,
> we dip to you, you will dip to us, Dionysus
> the plopping, pooling words, stirred
> by the lyre gaps between the peaks of flame,
> water to fire, us to them.

"The other great prehistoric invention came about when some
Paleolithic, lateral-thinking genius noticed that a twig which fell
into the grease below a roasting animal went on burning beyond
its natural span. From that observation, step by slow step, the idea
of the grease lamp evolved: first of a wick immersed in grease,
then of a portable container for the grease. The device had been
perfected at least 15,000 years ago since the painting in the
Lascaux cave in the Dordogne was illuminated by a hundred or
more grease lamps.

"Some primitive communities did not bother with making lamps;
they simply dried oily fish, stuck them in cleft sticks and lit them.
The Indians around Vancouver Island did this to the little
salmon-like candle fish, the Penobscot Indians used the sucker

fish, the New Zealand Maoris the mutton fish, the Newfoundlanders the dog fish. Oily birds got the same treatment: until late in the nineteenth century, Shetlanders used to catch stormy petrels, thread a fiber wick through them, stick the feet in a lump of clay and burn them as lamps; much earlier, the Danes had done the same with the Great Auk, using a moss wick stuck in the creature's oily belly. The simplest of all natural lamps was the firefly. The West Indians used to put them in wooden cages or even stick them with gum to their big toes in order to see snakes on the path at night. Anything for a light.

"By the time of classical Athens, domestic lighting was commonplace—fragments have been found of more than ten thousand lamps made between the first and third centuries BC— and the Romans were almost as addicted to artificial light as we are now. They set up factories to make pottery lamps in vast quantities both at home and throughout the empire. Even slaves had lamps: they used snail shells to hold the oil and a tow wick. The Romans also invented the candle, another great leap in lateral thinking: solid 'oil' instead of liquid made light truly portable and eliminated the expense of a container.

"Night life as an option democratically available to everyone, as a time when ordinary people can go about their ordinary business, give or take a few qualifications, is a relatively modern invention. Until less than two centuries ago, night was still a time of terrors, evil portents and violence, a no-go area where criminals, hobgoblins and all the other forces of darkness ruled, a time when law-abiding people bolted their doors and huddled together around the fire with only a candle to light them to bed.

"It was not until the introduction of gas lighting in the early nineteenth century that cities began to be illuminated regularly, reliably and on a large scale. London had gas lamps in the streets by 1807, Baltimore in 1816, Berlin in 1826.

"In January 1882, when someone threw the switch for the first street lamps... our perception of the world changed for good. Rayner Banham called it 'the greatest environmental revolution in human history since the domestication of fire.'

"According to the sociologist Murray Melbin, night is the last frontier and since the invention of artificial lighting we have colonized it in much the same way and in much the same spirit as the Americans colonized the West in the nineteenth century. Time is a dimension like space, says Melbin, and people have moved into the realm of night as the hours of daylight have become more congested... As Melbin sees it, night and day will soon be interchangeable; we have transformed our environment, so we will transform ourselves—physically, socially and psychologically—to fit the new 24-hour cycle of work.

"After the physical conquest of night, the search moved on into the inner darkness, the darkness inside the head. When Freud, defining the aim of psychoanalysis, said, 'Where the id was, there the ego shall be,' he was echoing, in his own way, God's first edict: 'Let there be light.'"

[18]

In the summer of 1996 I was left alone, without a light, for a half
hour, in Le Portel cave. Not a long time, but enough for my eyes
to become accustomed to total darkness. At first I closed my eyes
(wondering if it would make any difference; it didn't), and rubbed
my eyelids with my knuckles creating the dazzling diagrammatic
millrace known as phosphenes. Then I opened my eyes and stared
into the dark. After some ten minutes, pinpoints of light appeared
like a fine snowfall holding in place. I thought of the three levels
of light in the dark I felt myself inhabiting: the light in my head,
the light in cave dark, and the stars in the night sky above.

[19]

Herbert Kűhn, a German writer and the author of *On the Track of Prehistoric Man,* visited the Niaux cave in 1949. He believes that Niaux was one of the great religious centers for Ice Age people. At one point, he describes his feelings about The Green Lake, the underground siphon to the left of Niaux's second intersection:

> This lake is one of the most sinister things to be found in
> any of the subterranean grottoes, and when M. Clastres and
> I had reached it we sat down on a stone by its edge. Black
> and deathly quiet the waters stretched before us. The
> absolute stillness by the lakeside is so uncanny that it soon
> becomes almost unbearable. One is surrounded by
> premonitions of dread. Life is timeless and, what is more
> alarming, motionless. So profound is the quiet that one can
> feel one's very heartbeat. This sitting by the strand of a
> subterranean lake is a unique experience. There is always
> movement around us. Something or other is always
> happening. Even in the depths of the night there is noise.
> Leaves shiver, some beast will stir. You hear a house floor
> creak, you see the twinkling of a star, the wind comes
> blowing or a field mouse rustles in the grass. But by the
> banks of the pool in Niaux nothing stirs. If I had been alone
> on that occasion I believe that I would have broken down.
> Anxiety would have gripped me too tightly. A stillness, an
> immobility, a timelessness man cannot endure. And I could
> recollect the relief we felt when a drop of water plopped
> down from the vault above onto the surface of the lake.

Something had happened. A sense of salvation. Faint, circular ripples ringed outward toward the banks. Then again, all was still. So had the underground waters lain throughout the millennia: black, immobile, uncanny, awful.

[20]

Cold gibbons
nested fledglings
the crucified left for dead
cry out as one

or, as No One—if you're cyclopically listening.

[21]

Tracers 3

One day in the Dordogne there was a cool gray September flow
through the chestnuts, a leaf flutter so intense no single leaf could
be outlined. A dazzling like the sparking milling of cuneiform
fragments the backs of my hands release pressed against my
closed eyelids—all of which resolves into a doughnut of light,
with a cenote-black center, the outer ring of which appears fused
to astral dark. Is this the deep cone of the human, Giacometti-
wrapped in erasures, restarts and retreats?

*

We continue to be in multiphasic expulsion from a paradise we
unconsciously rejected when we separated ourselves from
animals. It took thousands and thousands of years but we did
create the abyss out of a seemingly infinitely elastic crisis: therio-
expulsion—and we have lived in a state of "animal withdrawal"
ever since. The pictures from the abyss that flicker our sleep and
waking are the fall-out that shouted us into dot and line and from
which we have been throwing up and throwing down ever since.

*

Bird spirit flew into Apollo—
animal appeared in Dis.

What was sky and earth became life and death,
or hell on earth and psychic depth,
and I wonder: how has Hades been affected by Dachau?
In the cold of deepest bowels, does a stained
fluid drip? Does pure loss now have an odor
of cremation, a fleshy hollow feel
of human soul infiltrating those realms
Hades had reserved for animals?
Are there archai, still spotted with
this evening's russets, stringing and quartering
an anthrobestial compost? Or are the zeros,
of which we are increasingly composed,
folding out the quick of animal life?
Is that why these outlines, these Hadic kin,
take on mountainous strength,
moving through the shadows of these days?

*

As if the night has tunnels that if tapped could lead one into the
recrementitious depths where Cro-Magnon dreams might be
envisioned... Were their dreams "open" in a way that ours are
not? The open Aurignacian vulva evokes a simple labyrinth with
an exit and stresses, sexually, torsion, possibly the earliest
intercourse/pregnancy association (underscored by the fire drill).
The subsequent uroboros belongs to agricultural peoples, with
stress on the enclosed seed, the male as "star," i.e., patriarchy in

contrast to an earlier more mysterious "open" union, in which the female was place-of-fire *and* phallus (the so-called "Venuses" fit neatly in the hand). Did Cro-Magnon people sense life as indeterminate, the human as unclosed? In Western symbolism, the circle is a symbol of death, or the wholeness that must include death… Cro-Magnon "death" as an absence containing a hidden presence to be drawn forth through stone.

[22]

E. M. Cioran:

"Two kinds of mind: daylight and nocturnal. They have neither
the same method nor the same morality. In broad daylight, you
watch yourself; in the dark, you speak out. The salutary or
awkward consequences of what he thinks matter little to the man
who questions himself at hours when others are the prey of sleep.
Hence he meditates upon the bad luck of being born without
concern for the harm he can cause others or himself. After
midnight begins the intoxication of pernicious truths.

"Once the shutters are closed, I stretch out in the dark. The outer
world, a fading murmur, dissolves. All that is left is myself and…
there's the rub. Hermits have spent their lives in dialogue with
what was most hidden within them. If only, following their
example, I could give myself up to that extreme exercise, in which
one unites with the intimacy of one's own being! It is this self-
interview, this inward transition which matters, and which has no
value unless continually renewed, so that the self is finally
absorbed by its essential version.

"Dreams, by abolishing time, abolish death. The deceased take
advantage of them in order to importune us. Last night, there was
my father. He was just as I have always known him, yet I had a
moment's hesitation. Suppose it wasn't my father? We embraced
in the Rumanian manner but, as always with him, without

effusion, without warmth, without the demonstrativeness customary in an expansive people. It was because of that sober, icy kiss that I knew it was my father. I woke up realizing that one resuscitates only as an intruder, as a dream-spoiler, and that such distressing immortality is the only kind there is.

"For Mallarmé, who claimed he was doomed to permanent insomnia, sleep was not a 'real need' but a 'favor.' Only a great poet could allow himself the luxury of such an insanity.

"The light of dawn is the true, primordial light. Each time I observe it, I bless my sleepless nights, which afford me an occasion to witness the spectacle of the Beginning. Yeats calls it 'sensuous'—a fine discovery, and anything but obvious.

"Much more than time, it is sleep that is the antidote to grief. Insomnia, on the other hand, which enlarges the slightest vexation and converts it into a blow of fate, stands vigil over our wounds and keeps them from flagging.

"'And God saw that the light was good': such is the opinion of mortals, with the exception of the sleepless, for whom it is an aggression, a new inferno more pitiless than the night's.

"I should like to forget *everything* and waken to a light *before time.*"

[23]

November 7, 1970   Methodist Hospital, Indianapolis

Walked into C 743. She was in a single railed bed, picking at
covers, trying to sit up—most of her hair gone—moth-eaten
stringy clumps sticking out straight—dyed-brown, skull showing.
Acorn, monkey: these words now cross my mind—then, to my
horror, I only saw my mother possibly mad in a short hospital
gown, sitting, helplessly picking at whatever, eyes wide, seeing,
not seeing, skull-head on tiny shoulders—legs bruised, dark
splotches, big feet, large dead toenails, legs like helpless clubs
sticking out.

We embraced—I held her a long time, a minute it seemed—two
minutes—she was a little crumpled and loosened pack of faggots.
I sat down, instant knowledge that she was my mother and also
no longer was—but she recognized me and told me, her mouth
and face slack and tense at once, that she was surprised and happy
to see me. I held her hand. Her grip strong two weeks ago was
somewhat gone, but her *fingers* held—sheer bone—her loose
skinned wrist mottled brown. I wanted to cry right off but kept
almost *savoring* the duality: this was the first time I had never
clearly seen her as my mother. In spite of her growing old, aging
until now did not essentially change her--even as she grew stiff,
and would walk leaning backwards, I still regarded her essentially
as I had from childhood, babyhood even, on----but today, at 5:00
PM Death had moved in—was now more than 51%? in and of
her. I thought immediately of Sam Abrams' youngest child

Joshua who at ten can't talk and has an acorn monkey fidgety muscle gesture look. Death as an interior other, coming alive— no—not *alive,* but as if, as a tree dies, *another* form of its withering emerges—as if dying/withering at a certain point becomes an image which is not simply the *loss* of life. This is horrible—more horrible than if I had walked into the room, saw her head bent over and she had looked up *without a face.* But it was not a blankness either that shook me—I couldn't say she had de-evolved and was now a wild child, or an animal crazed with disease in the woods. Again, that would have saved *me* from seeing *her.* No, it was my mother acting like a child—that is, she no longer had any protocol. She did not cross her legs, she had no underwear on and if I had tried to do so she would not have stopped me from looking at her cunt. Later she ate with her fingers and let me help her to the toilet. I lifted up the hospital gown and helped her sit down. In our whole life together I had never seen her undressed or had been with her while either of us performed a function in the bathroom. She was so out of it, so overtaken by biological ravage, that I had no context in which to place her. The *yet* that most profoundly resounds is: she was my mother. Death was Gladys Maine Spencer.

I sat down and held her hand. She again tried to get up into a sitting position, seemingly to read the hospital stamp on the sheet edge. I kept holding her hand and at a certain point my eyes were so flushed I let the cry come. I dropped her hand, buried my face in my own hands and wept. Not as long as when I realized in 1966 that I could not live with Barbara and Matthew, and not as convulsively. She patted my shoulder and said: "There, there, don't feel bad." I started to laugh in the midst of my tears, saying "You! You're telling *me* not to cry!" I awkwardly told her that I was crying because she was so sick. Then she said: "The greatest pleasure in my life has been to be your mother." I replied: "I *guess* (and I weighted that word) I've really liked being your son"—which I immediately corrected to: "I've *loved* being your son." Very quietly she said: "I know that." Then her mouth slacked and twitched, and she stared off, eyes wide open, into the dim wall…

I wish I could *render* her state more totally. I was struck by how her *otherness* was so close to that of many young people I've met briefly, when I have thought that they were out of it, drugs or whatever. When I finally made contact with the nurse, a very starched woman in her late 50s, squat and simplistic in the way she acted (telling my mother to be a "big girl"), she seemed just as out of it! After the nurse left, I helped my mother eat some of the smelly hospital fish they gave her. At one point, I looked out of the window and watched in the darkness seven stories below a large heavy black woman slowly cross the parking lot—*it's all dead*—that is the phrase that came to me, as if the nature of life—including the imagination that had opened to me when I was twenty-two— was that of death, as if that which lives and goes on is death. My mother was now a puppet, jerked by the cords of Death.

The shit on her hospital gown didn't upset me, nor did the single tooth that appeared to be the last one left in her mouth. It was when I *remembered*, thought of her as the person I had known more consequently than any other—thirty-five years—that I felt scared and sick. As long as I stayed in touch with what I immediately saw, I felt somewhat numb, as if memory is part of our lives and we repress whole memory out of not being able to stand the discrepancy between it and what we see. It was ok to watch her drowse. I was kind of charmed that she would eat with her fingers and would let me help her to the toilet with its frightening diagonal aluminum bar along the wall for the dying to grasp as they lowered themselves down.

[24]

I put my life into my mother's tomb. Her furniture: frozen animals. The atmosphere? I pulled the WC udder-chain of iron-geared clouds. It began to drizzle aftermath, inner math, registries of Wabash glades. Her bones, milk-soft, were xylophone to my mental tongs.

[25]

Djuna Barnes' Dr. Matthew-Mighty-grain-of-salt-Dante-O'Connor:

"We are but skin about a wind, with muscles clenched against mortality. We sleep in a long reproachful dust against ourselves. We are full to the gorge with our own names for misery.

"And the tree of night is the hardest tree to mount, the dourest tree to scale, the most difficult of branch, the most febrile to the touch, and sweats a resin and drips a pitch against the palm that computation has not gambled... We will find no comfort until the night melts away; until the fury of the night rots out its fire...

"For what is not the sleeper responsible? What converse does he hold and with whom? He lies down with his Nelly and drops off into the arms of his Gretchen. Thousands unbidden come to his bed. Yet how can one tell truth when it's never in the company?

"For the lover, it is the night into which his beloved goes that destroys his heart; he wakes her suddenly, only to look the hyena in the face that is her smile, as she leaves that company... When she sleeps, is she not moving her leg aside for an unknown garrison? Or in a moment, that takes but a second, murdering us with an axe? Eating our ear in a pie? Sailing to some port with a ship full of sailors and medical men?

"And so I say, what of the night, the terrible night? The darkness is the closet in which your lover roosts her heart, and that night-fowl that caws against her spirit and yours, dropping between you and her the awful estrangement of his bowels...

"To our friends, we die every day, but to ourselves we die only at the end. We do not know death, or how often it has essayed our most vital spirit. While we are in the parlour it is visiting in the pantry..."

[26]

Tracers 4

"It is clear," declared César Vallejo, noticing a black beetle giving head to a caiman virago, "why metaphysical life is so rich with pause."

*

Insomnia: trapped between the black wall inside my mind and the bedroom's darkness. I hang tracer after tracer upon this wall, as if to bring it down, but it regards these tracers as medals, expanding and thickening, proud of its valor...

*

Sudden image of the coal bin in my childhood home's basement where my father, with freshly-cut buckeye switch, took me one Sunday after lunch for having criticized that morning Reverend Ragan's sermon. I peer into the bin to discover in citrus-green light Hart Crane peering back... How do I know it is him? He has cauliflower ears...

*

Jazz improvisation relates to dream improvisation. Chord structure: the life under, directing the dream. No wonder the nighttime interest in jazz, the dream-fractured improvisational lines. "Koko" the ghost of "Cherokee," "Cherokee" the host of "Koko;" out of Charlie Parker's coke haven this mantic anthem. Walking on the gym track, listening to Sonny Stitt inject some "Koko" anti-freeze into my ear drums, I thought of the harp of baby birds plucked by Eve, the birth pangs of absence in every babe.

*

    In the neuron orgy
            in cranial dark
to know thyself is to give a self to no.

[27]

I was going many ways at once,
a drop of psyche had separated into streams,
each with a febrile image purpose,
ravenous image serpents all heading out hungry for extension,
one must choose
which serpent—or might one choose their knotted source?

One says: dream is a stable place to flail,
to swingle bast from circumstance

One says: dream wisps are image produce
the poet must pestle
or tie, dead giveaways

I am crawling a black alley past sights I cannot bear,
alley intestines, the monster composed of daily news

Last night a nipple was offered—
instead of sucking in the squalor discharge
I wrenched up, banging against
a ceiling roar of celebration

I looked back, the alley now spiraling to a vanishing

I was inside a Horn of Plenty with worm nests for the poor.
Where the fruits of the earth were said to spill,

a slab for the rich
barricaded the cornucopian flow.
Blood issued from the head of Achelous,
his horn ripped off by Heracles.
It is said that from the blood of this rupture
the Sirens were born—

ragged round pit of this tear:
does it mask the Muse's bloody mouth?

It is also said that Sirens were in the meadow with Kore,
bird-footed bearded girls
watching Kore pluck a psilocybin out of a cow-pie and bite
into the pileus

—I turned on the sink disposal and heard Kore's screams

Binder Siren, throttler Sphinx
cornucopia down into Muse eggs where inspiration
and fate separate and combine—

I keep having this fuzzy vision of
a brain termite queen pumping out image tendrils,
and then a creature blowing into it
(Sirens, the night-side of the ancient form of the Muse,
are said to suck the breath of the sick
and are associated with siesta-nightmares)
"muse" akin to *musus,*   "animal muzzle,"

a Muse-muzzled succubus crawling across the dreamer
or up through the dreaming,
blowing the dreamer's mind,
mind ejaculating into Muse muzzle,
"psyche" akin to "psychein" = to blow.

[28]

January 31, 1998. 8:16 AM. After writing my Notes, I assumed
From Scratch was finished and went to bed. I dreamed for hours
it seemed, over and over, of being at universities for poetry
readings. Each time I showed up for a reading I would discover
that I either had no books to read from, or that my books were in
foreign languages. At one point, someone handed me a copy of
The Gull Wall. Gratefully I opened it to discover words in
incoherent sentences instantly turning into other words. A 1950s
college audience was there, shuffling about, sitting down, getting
up, Cokes in hand. After five years, four thousand worksheets,
this dream... But are my books incomprehensible—is that the
message of this dream? You say that you write for yourself but
that you try hard to communicate this self to others. Maybe you
try too hard. Nobody wants all anybody else has. Are "alls"
poisoned, are some so heavy they feel like nothing? Is my all the
empty coal bucket Kafka's bucket rider mounts, or, in my case, a
book, there I am, riding my book about, hovering over a reader's
condo. Hello, I cry, it's me, Clayton E, I've just completed
another book! Another book, the interior groans, oh god he's
written another one. But no! This one is the best I've ever done,
this one will light up the distant horizon and demonstrate how
you are attached, or belong to that which is under you, this one
will point you at the looney tunes under all you think, Indiana to
Lascaux, one fast drive, a single smoking road.

[29]

I found myself yearning for the flutter folk, cordial nothing, the "is" without organs that so appeals to us.

Keep in change, reap falling—beautiful in the streetlight-lit night air: crystal down, dear fellow particles.

I had to come back to the Midwest to admire the separate isles of lacy structures as they mound on the redbud branch: mirth of the void, mouthlessly ho-hoing us...

What do these empty tree grails make of you? Who is your goddess? Are you the diamond nature?

As if the snow were a ludic mitten endlessly lolling...

As if what is invisible were mating with obliteration...

[30]

James Hamilton-Paterson:

"The famous and fatuous opposition of light and darkness is pre-
Socratic in origin, only one pair of many made up of a 'noble'
element (right, above, hot, male, dry, etc) and an 'ignoble' (left,
below, cold, female, wet). By the sixth and fifth centuries BC the
faculty of vision and the attributes of knowledge had run together
in the Greek word *theorein,* meaning both 'to see' and 'to know.'
Knowledge was henceforth a register of vision. Ignorance
therefore becomes a lack of knowledge predicated on objects not
being visible, so darkness equals ignorance. In turn, the dark
becomes a source of fear as if a knowledge of visible objects were
the only defense against terror and anxiety.

The very gradations of sleep itself seem to suggest a vertical
descent into annihilating depths, the deepest levels of sleep being
those of oblivion. The levels of dreaming, like the levels of the
ocean which can support the biggest life-forms, lie near the
surface. In any case, by descending into the sea we would expect
to meet the monstrous rather than the divine…. Astronauts have
claimed close encounters with a Supreme Being, but never deep-
sea divers. Nor should we be surprised. Superior beings are by
definition on top, while only the inferior can lurk below. The
deeps also remind us of where we suppose we originally came
from, what we have left behind. Going back to our genetic roots
rather than to the sunlit idyll of Eden is a disquieting affair. Did
we not abandon our ancestral dark by crawling toward the light?

No; we did not. The sea, to its dwellers, is not a dark place. With exceedingly acute eyes perceiving low levels of light and complex codes of bioluminescence; with sensitivity to sounds, smells, and minute pressure differentials far beyond the spectrum of our own senses, it is as pointless to speak in crude human terms of 'light' and 'dark' as it would be when speculating about what a bat sees. A bat 'sees' with its ears with great precision and at speed. In short there is no such thing as darkness. It exists only in the perception of the beholder. Vision does not depend on light."

[31]

Listening to Caryl sleep,
thinking of the cross-hatching in the 7-mile verticality of her
    living
as her mind makes its way across the 40,000-mile mid-ocean
    ridge,
across abyssal plains and canyons in tree-shaped networks,
her young life, which she remembers so keenly,
like a die tumbling among arabesques of leafy sea dragons trailing
kelp blends, green clouds pouring
from the sides of wounded fish, millions of image trains—
I am on one, looking down at the stratified carriers below,
one called Venus's-flower-basket, the passengers:
shrimp, crabs, worms, and clams. Multiple water spindles
    containing
water fairy proms, high school friends being reborn,
I am following the course of her sleep
through sea pastures of whirring diamond saws,
she carries away with her, in her trailing skirts,
a web filled with tiny men, radiolarian ooze,
at 800 feet, only the deepest, blackest blue,
the ocean of her sleep breaks over me, light gravel,
sensation of being in a horse's mouth, a deeper breathing is
    forming—
the infinite, far from being a suburb of the gods, is an eternal
surpassing, removed from any essential halt.
I see her standing before a glass stairway, a Jacob's ladder

with more steps than she could ever climb in three lifetimes,
they disappear like bubbles in champagne,
now she is struggling against
suctions and pulls, against stretched webs,
she breaks free—what nightmare did she just slip?—
she becomes navigation itself, shining with a pure white flame,
passing over foaming ditches, wheeling ravines,
I imagine her retinue: dwarf plankton, flamingo tongues,
coccoliths giving the water a milk glow, bristlefoooted worms
patterned with colored rosettes, salmon-pink winged slugs,
salps like little barrels, pulsating, a mouth at each end.
How do we do without a head? How present all edges of the
    body
equally to the outside world? A poem without subject,
all parts of which surprise and interlock, a poem with twenty
    centers,
all muscular and avid, each word dense, full in itself, a nest,
a sound of wood crackling in the fireplace, monkey words
feeling the earthquake coming before I do.
Going through myself,   is it her heart that I am hearing?
—she gasps—silence—rebreathes ka ka ka ka
suddenly she is other than herself,
rake tines rise from her brow projecting brain energy into the
    atmosphere,
impaling celestial hexes, they glow pale blue in the dark
like thin upraised arms; I pass slowly through them,
standing in my Protestant canoe, alone, stiff, an erection curving

from a golden pubic beard—behind my back:
the Absolute, straight as a wall.
I am possessed by a sole idea: that snow is ceaselessly falling
obliquely through all of us, on each flake
the population of the Beyond cluster
like minute beardless seals, or albino cougars,
spherical knots of unearthly calm... As my monoxylon
sinks slowly into dead space, the dark is flecked with one-winged
    birds,
barkless trees, and now I see the full squalor of the sea,
the rubbish of a thousand boats daily fished up, winnowed,
and thrown straight back—crushed into the netted haul
the new mermaid, limbs twisted among dogfish, whiting and
    plaice,
a deflated life-sized sex doll, hermit-crabs inside her
red-rimmed mouth. O sea layered into my dreams,
the daily rewound trash, visitations of the dead, Tenochtitlan
thoroughfares, extra-terrestrial spider queens,
cork-screwing flights through kaleidoscopic barriers—
to land by a nightstand and be watched by
two swans,   who are being watched by
two ocelots,   who are being watched by two snakes,   watched by
sixteen triangles,   watched by countless staring eyes.
Cessation of the mirage of the finite—
call it re-embarkation, call it a multiple leaving.
I have for shade a whole spread of hyena shadow,
I am my own ground, slashed, a wild sea of ground.

There is a silent breaking of waves,   spots of light,   sensation of
    fissure,
a flowing furrow,   I see Caryl gliding through
the little curlicues in its flanks,
and when I graze her I graze a deep pit of joy.

[December-February, 2010/2011]

Clayton Eshleman's most recent publications include *The Complete Poetry of César Vallejo* (University of California Press, 2007), *The Grindstone of Rapport / A Clayton Eshleman Reader* (Black Widow Press, 2008), *Anticline* (Black Widow Press, 2010), *Solar Throat Slashed* (a translation of Aimé Césaire's *Soleil cou coupé*, with A. James Arnold, Wesleyan University Press, 2011), and *Endure* (a selected translations of Bei Dao, with Lucas Klein, Black Widow Press, 2011). Eshleman is the first poet to realize a huge, researched, and imaginative project, in prose and poetry, on Ice Age cave art: *Juniper Fuse: Upper Paleolithic Imagination & the Construction of the Underworld* (Wesleyan University Press, 2003). He was also the founder and editor of *Caterpillar* magazine (1967-1973) and *Sulfur* magazine (1981-2000). He continues to live with his wife Caryl in Ypsilanti, Michigan.